Comparing Bugs

Bug Homes

Charlotte Guillain

Heinemann Library
Chicago, Illinois

www.heinemannraintree.com

Visit our website to find out more information about Heinemann-Raintree books.

To order:

☎ Phone 888-454-2279

💻 Visit www.heinemannraintree.com to browse our catalog and order online.

Edited by Rebecca Rissman and Catherine Veitch
Designed by Joanna Hinton-Malivoire
Picture research by Elizabeth Alexander
Production by Duncan Gilbert and Victoria Fitzgerald
Originated by Heinemann Library
Printed and bound in China by South China Printing Company Ltd

14 13 12 11 10
10 9 8 7 6 5 4 3 2 1

Library of Congress Cataloging-in-Publication Data
Bug homes / Charlotte Guillain. -- 1st ed.
p. cm. -- (Comparing bugs)
ISBN 978-1-4329-3568-9 (hb) -- ISBN 978-1-4329-3577-1 (pb)
QL467.2.G8564 2010
595.7156'4--dc22
                    2009025550

Acknowledgments

The author and publishers are grateful to the following for permission to reproduce copyright material: Alamy pp. **11** (© Roger Eritja), **12** (© Manor Photography), **20** (© Emir Shabashvili), **14** (© cbimages); Capstone Global Library pp. **18** (Steven Mead), **23 top** (Steven Mead); Corbis pp. **5** (© Theo Allofs/zefa), **16** (© William Radcliffe/Science Faction); FLPA p. **17** (© Konrad Wothe/Minden Pictures), Photolibrary pp. **4** (Don Johnston/All Canada Photos), **7** (Michael Fogden/OSF), **10** (Oxford Scientific), **8** (Paul Freed/Animals Animals), **9** (David M Dennis/Animals Animals), **19** (Clarence Styron/age footstock), **15** (Polka Dot Images), **23 middle bottom** (David M Dennis/Animals Animals); Shutterstock pp. **6** (© Styve Reineck), **13** (© David Lee), **21** (© Florin Tirlea), **22 top left** (© alle), **22 bottom left** (© Levitskiy Nikolay), **22 top right** (© aaaah), **22 bottom right** (© Eric Isselée), **23 bottom** (© Florin Tirlea), **23 middle top** (© David Hughes).

Cover photograph of a beehive reproduced with permission of Shutterstock (©Subbotina Anna). Back cover photograph of termite hills reproduced with permission of Shutterstock (© Styve Reineck).

The publishers would like to thank Nancy Harris and Kate Wilson for their assistance in the preparation of this book.

Every effort has been made to contact copyright holders of any material reproduced in this book. Any omissions will be rectified in subsequent printings if notice is given to the publisher.

Contents

Meet the Bugs

There are many different types of bugs.

Bugs live in many different types of homes.

On and In the Ground

Some termites build homes out of mud.

tunnels

Termites make tunnels in their homes.

Some centipedes live in soil.

Earthworms make tunnels in soil.

On Water

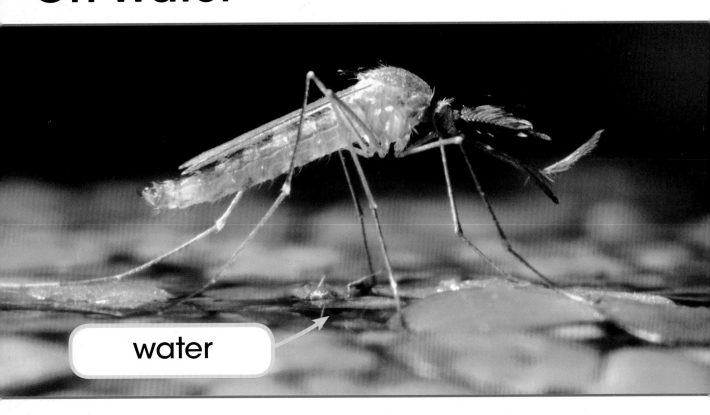

water

Some insects live on water.

eggs

Some insects lay their eggs in water.

Wood

Many insects live in wood.

Many wood lice live under logs.

Plants

leaf

Some insects live on leaves.

stick insect

Some insects live in trees
and bushes.

Webs and Nests

web

Spiders make webs from silk.

Some spider webs are like tunnels.

nest

Some caterpillars make nests from silk.

nest

Some wasps make nests from plants they eat.

nest

Honeybees make nests out of wax.

The honeybees live in the nest.

How Big?

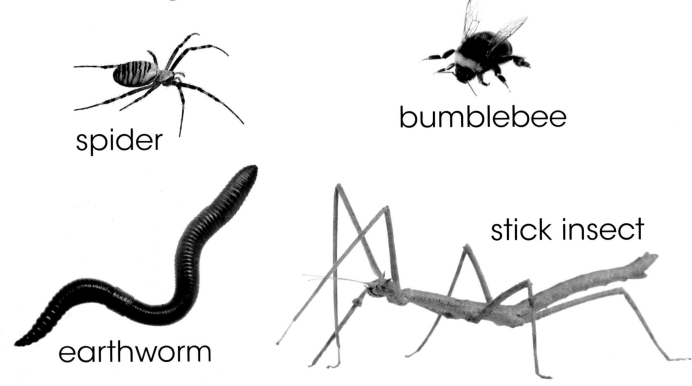

spider

bumblebee

stick insect

earthworm

Look at how big some of the bugs in this book can be.

Picture Glossary

 **silk** soft, strong material

 **soil** top layer of ground that you can grow plants in

 **tunnel** long underground passageway

 **wax** sticky yellow material

Index

Notes to Parents and Teachers
Before reading
Make a list of bugs with the children. Try to include insects, arachnids (e.g. spiders), crustaceans (e.g. wood lice), myriapods (e.g. centipedes and millipedes), and earthworms. Ask the children if they know where any of these bugs live. What sort of homes do bugs make for themselves?

After reading
- Go on a hunt for spider webs – a good time to do this is on a misty morning. Where do spiders make their webs? Take photographs of the webs you find and look at them together on the interactive whiteboard. Look at the structure of the webs carefully. Try making a web together with string on the classroom wall. Is this easy to do?
- Take the children to hunt for other bugs. Help them to peel back bark on rotten logs, look under stones, look for worms in soil, or find caterpillars on leaves. Draw up tally charts with the children to record how many different places bugs were found.
- Read the children *The Very Busy Spider* by Eric Carle.